Crafts for All Seasons

by Tania Kourempis-Cowling

About the Author

Tania Kourempis-Cowling is an educational writer specializing in activities for the early childhood student. Many of these ideas have been taken from her "Learning by Doing" column that appeared in the <u>Doings Newspaper</u> in Illinois. She enjoys planning activities for parents and children, as well as teachers and students. She writes articles for many teaching publications and has authored a previous book called <u>Shake, Tap and Play a Merry Tune</u> (Fearon).

To my husband John, whose love, patience, and support has made this book possible.

Senior Editor: Kristin Eclov
Cover and Interior Design: Good Neighbor Press, Inc.
                           Grand Junction, CO
Interior Illustration: Corbin Hillam

© Fearon Teacher Aids
A Division of Frank Schaffer Publications, Inc.
23740 Hawthorne Boulevard
Torrance, CA 90505-5927

FE7950
ISBN 1-56417-950-8

2 3 4 5 6 7 8 9

Table of Contents

Introduction

Every season brings opportunities to present fun activities to children. This book is composed of art activities that teach seasonal weather changes as well as explore different holidays. Art is so important in developing imagination, individuality, and aesthetic appreciation. It is a good release for emotions, as well as a toner for eye-hand coordination.

Children learn by doing. Through careful planning and flexibility with the creative process, you can provide an environment of fun. Though I have patterned ideas on each page, encourage each child to express themselves with as much creativity as possible. Remember that the process is more important than the finished product.

Fall

Another word for fall is autumn. It begins each year with the autumnal equinox, which is late September. It is the season between summer and winter when the leaves change color and fall from the trees. Fall is a time for harvesting food and preparing for the cold months to come. It is a special time when school begins.

6

Foil Leaves

Tools and Materials

Aluminum foil
Leaves
Crayons
Construction paper
Tape

Activity

Cut a piece of aluminum foil about 4" x 4" (10cm x 10cm) or larger than leaves you've collected for this project. The foil can be cut in any shape as long as it covers the leaf. Place the foil over a fall leaf. Gently rub crayons over the foil to get the leaf print. Mount this foil leaf onto a 9" x 12" (22.5cm x 30cm) construction-paper frame with tape.

Note: Use several crayons in the fall colors of red, yellow, orange, and brown.

7

Texture Tree

Tools and Materials

Poster board or heavy construction paper
Crayons and markers
Scissors
Fabrics

Activity

Draw a tree trunk on heavy construction paper or poster board. Color it brown with crayons or markers. Cut leaves from various fabrics, such as flannel, burlap, corduroy, faux fur, velvet, nylon netting, etc. Glue these leaves onto the tree.

Tree Mosaic

Tools and Materials

Poster board
Glue
Dried beans—black beans, yellow and green split peas, red
  beans, lentils

Activity

Draw a tree-shape on poster board. Spread glue onto the
tree. Glue black beans on the trunk. Using different colored
beans, glue them on as fall leaves. Put a few colored beans
around the bottom of the tree to show some fallen leaves.

Variation: Kidney beans can be glued among the leaves to
look like apples.

9

Apple Collage

Tools and Materials

Small paper plate
Red construction paper or tissue paper
Green construction paper
Glue

Activity

Use a small paper plate as your apple form. Tear small pieces of red construction paper and glue these onto the plate. Overlap the pieces slightly, and fully cover the plate. Add a green construction-paper stem.

Variation: Pieces of red tissue paper can be used for a more transparent look.

Apple Prints

Tools and Materials

Shallow pan
Two apples
Red poster paint
Construction paper
Knife
Green marker

Activity

Prepare a shallow pan with red poster paint. You will need two apples. Cut one lengthwise to view the apple and its core. The other apple should be cut in half, horizontally. The star pattern will appear. Dip the apples into the paint, and print them on construction paper. Use green markers to add leaves and stems.

Variation: This project can also be done with a potato. Cut a potato in half. Carve a design out, leaving some raised parts. Dip it into the paint, and print it on paper.

11

Little Brown Squirrel

Tools and Materials

Poster board
Plastic egg-shaped hosiery container
Brown tissue paper
Glue
Markers
Construction paper
Scissors

Activity

Create a circle base from a ¾" x 8" (1.9cm x 20 cm) strip of cardboard or poster board. Make a tail from brown construction paper by cutting a large oval and fringing the edges. Staple the tail to the circle base.

For the squirrel's body, use a plastic hosiery container. Paint this egg with thin glue and cover it with pieces of brown tissue paper. Overlap the egg with pieces until the entire surface is covered. Again, paint over the egg with glue to secure all the tissue paper. When thoroughly dry, add facial features with a marker.

Note: Brown tissue paper can be purchased at art supply stores and most greeting-card stores.

Our Family Tree

Tools and Materials

White construction paper
Green, yellow, and red construction paper
Crayons and markers
Scissors
Glue

Activity

Encourage the children to chat with family members to learn about loved ones in the past. The family tree can go back as far into the past as you wish.

Draw a tree with branches on a 9" x 12" (22.5cm x 30cm) sheet of white construction paper. Color the trunk and branches brown. Make a name tag from construction paper and print the child's name on it. Glue it in the center of the tree. Cut leaf shapes from green, yellow, and red construction paper. Print the names of the grandparents from both sides of the family on one color of the leaves. Glue these onto the tree together, with one family on each side of the tree. Next, print the names of the child's parents on another color of leaves. Glue them on the tree near their parents. Last, print names of all the siblings on another color of leaves. Glue them on the tree near the parents. You now have a family tree in the colors of fall.

13

Button Trees

Tools and Materials

Denim or heavy fabric
Craft glue
Scissors
Buttons
Ribbon

Activity

Cut a tree shape from heavy fabric. Ask each child to bring buttons from home, preferably buttons cut from old clothing. Decorate the trees by gluing on these buttons. Punch a hole at the top of the tree and thread a ribbon to use as a hanger. This will make a cute ornament to use on the family Christmas tree or just to hang at any time as a decoration.

Our Family Bookmark

Tools and Materials

Construction paper
Clear adhesive paper
Markers and crayons
Stickers

Activity

Cut the construction paper into 3" x 9" (7.5cm x 22.5cm) strips—a typical bookmark size. Instruct the students to decorate one side of the bookmark and write the words "Our Family." Encourage the children to take the bookmark home and ask all their family members to sign their names on the back. Bring the bookmark back to class and laminate it in plastic. This makes a memorable and useful gift for any family member.

15

Picture Puzzle

Tools and Materials

Photo of child
Poster board
Glue or spray adhesive
Crayon or marker
Scissors
Envelope

Activity

Use a photocopier to enlarge the photo of the child to 8½" x 11" (21.3cm x 27.5cm). Glue this page to poster board. When the page is fully dry, use a crayon or marker to draw puzzle-shaped pieces on the back. With scissors, cut along these lines to make puzzle pieces. Put all the pieces in an envelope. Address the envelope to a relative and mail it to him or her. It's a fun way to receive a new photo.

Walnut Boats

Tools and Materials

Half walnut shells
Clay
Toothpicks
White construction paper
Nutcracker

Activity

Fill the walnut shell with clay. Cut out ship sails from white construction paper. Thread a toothpick in and out of the paper sail as shown. Stick the toothpick end in the clay. In a large container of water, encourage the children to sail their boats on the ocean as Columbus did.

17

Ship in a Bottle

Tools and Materials

Plastic food wrap or cellophane
Blue and white construction paper
Crayons
Glue
Scissors
Tape

Activity

Cut a large bottle shape from white construction paper. With crayons, draw a picture of one of Columbus' ships. Cover the picture with plastic wrap. Tape the wrap on the back of the picture. This will look like the ship is contained in the glass bottle. Glue the finished bottle onto a 9" x 12" (22.5cm x 30cm) sheet of blue construction paper.

Classroom Garland

Tools and Materials

Construction paper
Scissors
Stapler
Crepe-paper streamers

Activity

String crepe-paper streamers around the room. Encourage the children to draw and cut out paper ships, telescopes, and flags. Attach the artwork to the crepe-paper streamers to decorate the classroom for Columbus Day.

Halloween Bat

Tools and Materials

Cardboard toilet-paper tube
Orange tempera paint
Black construction paper
Glue
Scissors
Black marker or crayon

Activity

Paint the cardboard tube orange—it represents the bat's body. Cut five 1-inch (2.5cm) wide strips from black construction paper. Glue three strips to the back of the tube, and center them to become the wings. Accordion pleat two construction-paper strips, and glue them to the bottom of the tube. These are the bat's legs. Cut two pointed ears and glue these to the top of the tube as his ears. Add facial features with a black marker or crayon.

20

Foam Skeletons

Tools and Materials

Black construction paper
S-shaped and round foam packing pieces
Glue
Construction-paper scraps (all colors)

Activity

Create a night picture on a large sheet of black construction paper. Use different colored construction-paper scraps to make buildings, landscaping, and a bright moon. Use the foam packing pieces to create jointed skeletons floating across the sky. Glue all the pieces into place on the paper.

21

Clothespin Bat

Tools and Materials

Spring-type clothespins
Black craft or tempera paint
Black construction paper or poster board
Glue

Activity

Paint a spring-type clothespin with black paint. This is the bat's body. Cut wings from black construction paper or poster board. Use the pattern provided or try it freehand. Glue the wings to the back of the clothespin. Now, the children can clip these bats onto objects around the classroom or take them home for decoration.

pattern

Reproducible

Ghost Necklaces

Tools and Materials

Black and orange poster board
Dried lima beans
Markers
Glue
Yarn

Activity

Cut the black or orange poster board into circles measuring about 3 inches (7.5cm) in diameter. Use dried lima beans to represent little ghosts. Draw on eyes and mouths with a black marker. Glue the ghosts randomly on the poster-board circles. When dry, punch two holes at the top of the circles and thread with yarn for a necklace.

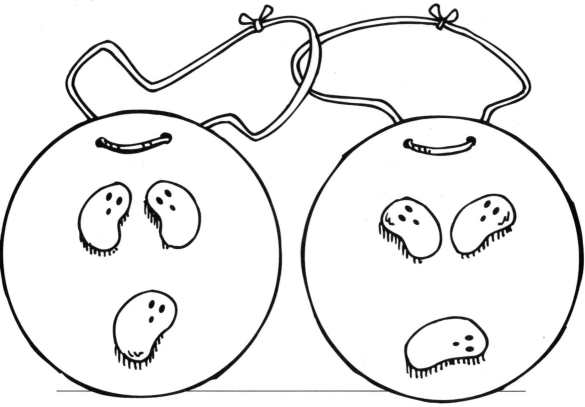

3-D Turkey

Tools and Materials

Brown construction paper or brown paper bag
Light-colored sheet of construction paper
Construction paper (all colors)
Tape
Glue
Scissors
Markers

Activity

Cut out a turkey body from brown construction paper (a small scale pattern is shown). Glue the turkey onto the sheet of light-colored construction paper. Cut strips of construction paper about 1" x 4" (2.5cm x 10cm) in a wide variety of colors. Make a circular loop from each strip of paper and tape the ends together. Glue the loops onto the turkey to create a three-dimensional span of tail feathers. Use markers to draw an eye, two feet, and a red wattle.

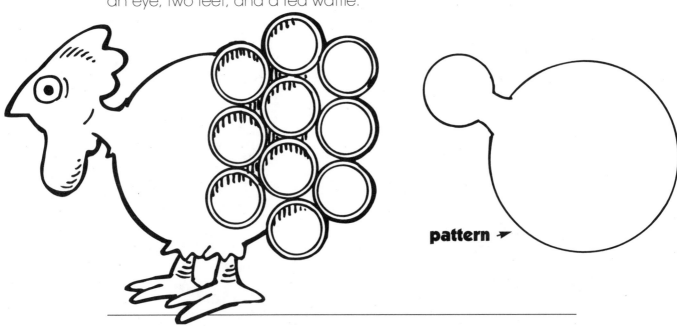

pattern ➤

24

Reproducible

Indian Corn Art

Tools and Materials

Graph paper
Crayons or markers
Brown shopping bag
Scissors

Activity

Cut out corn-cob shapes from graph paper. Use crayons or markers, in orange, yellow, brown, and red, to color the squares in a random design. Make a paper corn husk from brown grocery bags for each corn cob. Arrange the cobs into clusters. Use the corn-cob art to decorate the room.

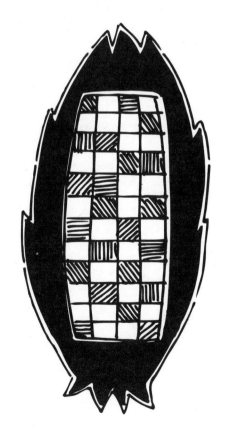

Spicy Pies

Tools and Materials

Orange and brown construction paper
Glue
Whole cloves
Cinnamon
Ginger

Activity

Cut circles about 4 inches (10cm) in diameter, from orange and brown construction paper. Brush the surface of the circle with glue. Arrange the cloves in any design, then sprinkle with cinnamon and ginger. These make fragrant pies to decorate the classroom.

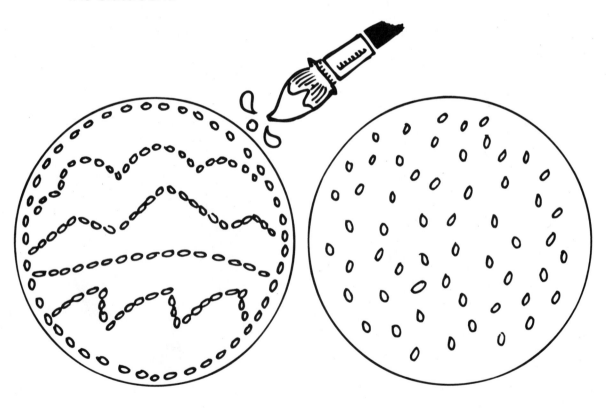

26

Pleated Turkey

Tools and Materials

Orange, brown, and red construction paper
Staples or tape
Scissors
Glue

Activity

Accordion pleat a 9" x 12" (22.5cm x 30cm) sheet of orange
construction paper. Fold the pleated paper in half and staple
the center pleats together. From brown construction paper,
cut a 4-inch (10cm) circle for the turkey body and a 1½-inch
(3.75cm) circle for the head. From red construction paper cut
a wattle (see pattern). Glue the turkey together as shown.
Next, use a marker to draw the eyes and beak. Finally, glue
the tail to the back of the body. Decorate the classroom with
these turkeys by taping them to walls and windows and
hanging them from the ceiling.

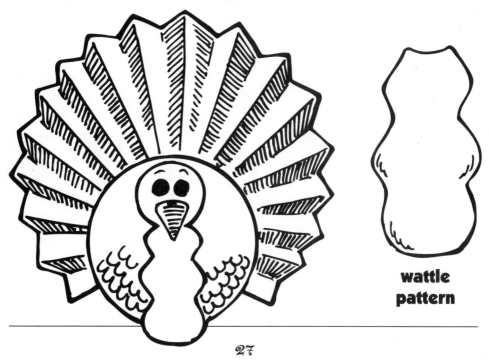

**wattle
pattern**

27

Reproducible

Popcorn Mosaic

Tools and Materials

Colored popcorn kernels
Glue
Cardboard

Activity

Supermarkets and specialty shops now sell popcorn kernels that have been dyed a variety of colors. Using these kernels, glue them onto cardboard creating colorful designs and pictures. Try designs, such as the pictures shown below.

Hand Turkeys

Tools and Materials

Construction paper
Crayons and markers
Tempera paint (optional)

Activity

Trace each child's hand on construction paper, making sure that the fingers are spread apart. Encourage the children to color each finger like a turkey's bright tail feather. Color the palm of the hand and the thumb brown for the turkey's body and head. Use markers to draw features, such as the eye, beak, and wattle.

To make a greeting card, fold construction paper in half. Draw the hand turkey on the cover and print this cute verse inside.

This is a turkey picture,
As you can plainly see.
I made it with my hand,
Which is a part of me.
It comes with special thoughts,
Especially to say.
I hope you have a very happy Thanksgiving Day!

Variation: Print a hand turkey with tempera paint. Apply a thin coat of paint to the child's hand with a brush or sponge. Have the child press down with his or her hand on the paper for a print. Add features as above.

29

Winter

Winter usually begins around December 21st. It is the season between autumn and spring. In many parts of the world the weather becomes very cold and the ground is covered with ice and snow. Winter is a time when people wear heavier clothes and animals either adapt to the cold or hibernate until spring.

Honeycomb Snowflake

Tools and Materials

Paper plate
Blue tempera poster paint
Paintbrush
Honeycomb Cereal™
Glue
Silver glitter

Activity

Paint the surface of one paper plate blue. Make a snowflake by gluing Honeycomb™ cereal pieces together on the paper plate. Brush or lightly spread glue on the cereal pieces and sprinkle with silver glitter.

Caution: Supervise young children very closely when using glitter.

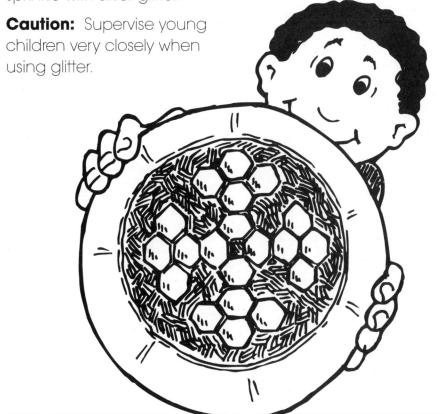

31

Snow-Soap Painting

Tools and Materials

Ivory™ soap flakes
Warm water
Hand or electric beater
Dark-colored construction paper
Tools to apply paint
Craft stick

Activity

Mix 1 cup (240ml) Ivory™ Soap Flakes with ½ cup (120ml) of warm water in a large bowl. Use a hand beater or an electric mixer and whip until the mixture is fluffy. Make a winter picture using this snow-textured paint on dark-colored construction paper. Instead of paintbrushes, use craft sticks, plastic eating utensils, and toothbrushes, to apply the soapy paint. Allow the picture to dry thoroughly before hanging it as a winter decoration.

Hanukkah Menorah

Tools and Materials

12" x 4" (30cm x 10cm) Wood or cardboard platform
Ten wooden or plastic thread spools
Glue
Gold or silver spray paint
Small birthday candles

Activity

The menorah is a nine-branched candlestick made of wood, brass, silver, or gold. In the center of the menorah is the "shamash," which is taller than the other candles. Each of the eight nights of Hanukkah, a candle is lit from the shamash going from left to right.

Glue eight spools onto the platform, leaving space in the middle for one taller spool, to represent the "shamash." To create the taller spool, glue one spool on top of another, then glue it to the middle of the platform. Spray paint the menorah with gold or silver paint. Place small purchased candles into each spool's center.

33

Hanukkah Puzzles

Tools and Materials

A picture of a menorah, Star of David, or any Hanukkah picture
Cardboard
Glue
Clear adhesive paper
Scissors

Activity

Measure and cut the cardboard and Hanukkah picture the same size. Glue the picture onto the cardboard and laminate it with clear adhesive paper. Cut the picture into assorted puzzle pieces. The puzzle can be stored in a plastic bag or box for later use.

Hanukkah Pretzels

Tools and Materials

Thick pretzel logs
Milk chocolate chips
Wax paper
Microwave oven
Yellow candy sprinkles

Activity

Pour the bag of chocolate chips into a bowl and melt it in a microwave oven. Stir until soft and smooth. Dip about ⅓ of each pretzel log into the chocolate and sprinkle with yellow candy sprinkles. Place these on wax paper to set, about one hour. These tasty treats resemble Hanukkah candles. Enjoy!

35

Potato Art

Tools and Materials

Potatoes
Poster paint
Shallow container
Paper
Plastic knife

Activity

Cut a potato in half. On the inside draw a Hanukkah design, like a Star of David. Using a plastic knife cut away the excess potato around the design. Pour paint into a shallow container. Dip the potato into the paint or brush the paint onto the potato design. Press the potato on paper to make a print. The child can make repeated images on paper.

Note: The children should be very closely supervised when cutting the potatoes. Or cut out the designs in advance.

36

3-D Holiday Tree

Tools and Materials

Cardboard toilet- or paper-towel rolls
Glue
Stapler
Scissors
Tempera paint
Miniature pompoms, ornaments, marbles, etc.

Activity

Cut the cardboard tubes into 1-inch (2.5cm) rings. Paint each ring with green tempera paint. Glue or staple the cardboard rings together to form a triangular tree shape. Decorate the tree by placing a pompom or miniature ornament inside each ring.

Variation: Hanukkah bushes can be made using the same technique. Use blue paint instead of green. Decorate the inside rounds with Stars of David made from aluminum foil.

37

Macaroni Wreath

Tools and Materials

Paper plate
Uncooked macaroni—any shape(s) of your choice
Crepe paper, yarn or ribbon bow
Gold or green spray paint
Glue

Activity

Begin by cutting out the center of the paper plate, leaving a ring that is 3 inches (7.5cm) wide. Glue macaroni shapes onto the wreath shape. Once the glue is dry, spray paint the entire surface. Allow the wreath to dry before handling. Then attach a pretty bow and hang in a favorite place.

Variation: Paint the wreath green, then glue round cereal as the ornaments. Attach a pretty bow.

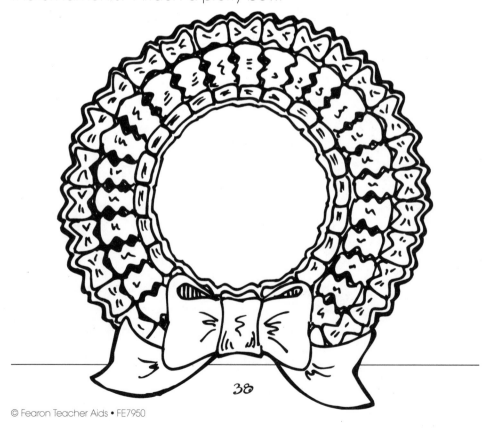

38

Paper-Plate Santa

Tools and Materials

White paper plates
Crayons or markers
Glue
Cotton balls

Activity

Use one whole paper plate for Santa's head. Draw the eyes, nose, mouth and rosy cheeks onto the center part of the paper plate. Glue cotton balls on for Santa's eyebrows and mustache.

Cut out Santa's hat from the center of another paper plate. Color it red and staple it to the top of his head. Cut one piece of a paper-plate rim and glue it to the base of the hat for the trim. Attach a cotton ball to the top of the hat as a pompom. Cut off the rims from several white paper plates and cut them into pieces. Overlap and glue the plate pieces all around Santa's face to create his beard. Allow the face to dry before handling.

39

Tree Ornament

Tools and Materials

White or green poster board
Crayons, markers, paints, glitter, sequins, etc.
Glue
Spring-type clothespin

Activity

Cut a Christmas-tree shape from poster board. Decorate the tree with crayons, markers, paints, glitter, sequins, etc. Glue a spring-type clothespin to the back of the tree. Make sure the bottom of the tree is close to the clip part. Clip the ornament onto a branch of a Christmas tree.

Another fun way to use the tree is to clip it to your coat lapel and wear it like a Christmas pin.

Rigatoni Wreath

Tools and Materials

Rigatoni macaroni
Red and green food coloring
Wax paper
Curling ribbon
Scissors

Activity

Dip rigatoni in food-colored water. Place the dyed macaroni on wax paper to dry. Thread curling ribbon through three to five pieces of rigatoni. Tie the strands together and curl the ribbons by pulling ends over a blade of scissors. Use the rigatoni wreaths as ornaments on a tree or decorations in the classroom.

41

Angel

Tools and Materials

Toilet-paper tube
White construction paper
Chenille stem
Glue
Markers or crayons

Activity

Draw a face on one end of a cardboard tube. Trace and cut out the angel-wing pattern (pattern shown) from white construction paper. Glue the wings to the back of the tube. Make a halo by bending one end of a chenille stem into a circle. Bend the halo forward and glue it to the top of the tube.

pattern

42

Reproducible

Stained-Glass Candle

Tools and Materials

Baby food jar
Dilluted white glue or liquid starch
Tissue paper (all colors)
Paintbrush
Small votive candle
Thin ribbon

Activity

Paint the outside of a baby-food jar with liquid starch or dilluted white glue. Using a variety of colors, stick pieces of torn tissue paper onto the jar surface. Do not extend the pieces beyond the rim. Brush a second coat of starch or glue on the covered jar. Allow the jar to dry thoroughly. Tie a thin ribbon around the top and place a small votive candle inside. Assist the children with lighting these candles and enjoy the beautiful holiday glow. These make wonderful gifts from the children to family members.

43

Musical-Note Ornament

Tools and Materials

Heavy black construction paper or poster board
Face photo of each child
Hole punch
Yarn or ribbon

Activity

Cut out a musical-note shape from heavy black paper or poster board for each child. Teach the children about the different types of musical notes by using whole, half, quarter, eighth and sixteenth note shapes. Glue each child's photo in the center of a musical note. Punch a hole at the top and add a ribbon or yarn hanger.

44

Place Mat (Mᶜkeka)

Tools and Materials

White construction paper
1" x 2" (2.5cm x 5cm) square sponges
Red, green, and black poster paints
Paper towels
Three shallow containers

Activity

During Kwanzaa this special placemat is the first object put on the holiday table. Make this fun replica design using a sponge-paint technique.

Pour each paint into a shallow container. Give each child three sponge squares. Using one sponge per color, dip the sponge into the paint. Dab the excess paint on the paper towel or gently scrape it on the side of the container. Press the paint side of the sponge onto the paper. Repeat the square pattern one after another in strips. Alternate the colors to make a block-print design.

45

Flag Cookies

Tools and Materials

Graham crackers
Vanilla frosting
Food coloring

Activity

Each graham-cracker cookie will make one flag with Kwanzaa colors. Divide the frosting into three bowls. Add food coloring to make red, green, and black frosting. Frost each graham cracker making equal size stripes of each color. Use red on the top, black in the center, and green on the bottom. Serve these as a snack on the days of Kwanzaa from December 26 through January 1.

46

Ears of Corn (Vibunzi)

Tools and Materials

Brown grocery bag
Yellow, orange, and red construction paper
Glue

Activity

Cut shapes like ears of corn from brown, grocery bags. Tear or cut small square pieces from colored construction paper. Glue the colored squares in rows, like kernels, on the paper ear of corn. Alternate the kernel colors to look like fall corn.

Note: Ears of corn symbolize the children in the home during Kwanzaa.

47

New Year's Hat

Tools and Materials

Construction paper (any color)
Crayons or markers
Thin elastic

Activity

Discuss with the children that New Year's resolutions provide a way to a good start for the coming year. People promise to do things better and in a different way. For example, a child's resolution may be to read a book a week, keep her desk neat, or feed the family pet. Encourage the children to write a list of three to five resolutions.

Roll a 12" x 18" (30cm x 45cm) sheet of construction paper into a cone shape. Mark where the papers overlap. Lay the paper flat. On the unmarked area draw pictures and write the promises. Roll the paper into the cone shape and staple it together. Punch a hole on each side of the cone. Thread a thin piece of elastic through each hole and knot it to keep the hat under the child's chin.

Kazoo Horns

Tools and Materials

Paper-towel tubes
Wax paper
Wide rubber band
Colored foil or aluminum foil
Ribbons and streamers
Glue
Permanent markers

Activity

Cover one end of a paper-towel tube with a piece of wax paper and secure it with a wide rubber band. Glue or tape colored foil around the tube. Glue on ribbons or streamers. Use markers to write "Happy New Year!" on the foil. To play, hum into the open end. Make loud sounds or hum a familiar tune.

49

Tin Noisemakers

Tools and Materials

Two aluminum pie plates—small or regular
Dried beans
Crayons, stickers, acrylic paints, etc.
Paper streamers
Tape

Activity

Place dried beans in one pie plate and invert the second plate over the first. Tape the two pie plates together. Decorate the plates with crayons, stickers, and acrylic paints. Attach paper streamers to the center of one plate with tape. Shake, shake, shake for a Happy New Year!

50

Paper-Plate Shaker

Tools and Materials

Plastic sandwich bag
Dried beans or popcorn
Paper plate
Stapler
Glue
Tongue depressor or craft stick
Markers, stickers, streamers, etc.

Activity

Partially fill a plastic bag with dried beans or popcorn kernels. Staple the bag securely to the bottom half of a paper plate. Glue a tongue depressor or craft stick to the same half of the paper plate. Fold the top half of the plate over the bag and staple the paper-plate edges together. Decorate the shaker with markers, stickers, and streamers. Now, shake, shake, shake—a great party craft!

51

Year's Past Quilt

Tools and Materials

White drawing paper
Fabric crayons
Plain fabric (muslin or cotton)
Permanent markers

Activity

Take a sheet of drawing paper and fold it to make six equal boxes. Using fabric crayons, invite each child to draw six things he or she remembers from the past year. For example, a family vacation, trip to the zoo, or a birthday celebration.

Transfer the drawings by placing the paper face down on a slightly larger piece of fabric then press with a hot iron. Make dots or Xs with a permanent marker to give the appearance of stitching.

This masterpiece is to hang up or frame.

52

Blizzard Art

Tools and Materials

Dark blue or black construction paper
Construction paper scraps
Aluminum foil
White tempera paint
Sponge
Glue

Activity

On a dark blue or black sheet of construction paper, create a street of houses. Using colorful construction paper, cut geometric shapes to make houses and glue them to the paper. Cut pieces of aluminum foil into small squares and glue them to the houses to create windows. Cut out other shapes from construction paper to look like trees and sidewalks. Glue them in place. When your city block is finished, sponge paint a white blanket of snow on roofs, trees, and ground for a snowstorm effect.

Marbled Mittens

Tools and Materials

White construction paper
Aluminum pie plate
Marbles
Tempera paint
Scissors
Yarn or ribbon
Stapler or tape

Activity

Cut white construction paper into mitten shapes. Place one mitten into an aluminum pie plate. In another container, put a few marbles into tempera paint. Spoon out the paint-covered marbles and place them on top of the mitten shape. Carefully roll the marbles over the mitten for a unique pattern design. Do the same procedure for the other mitten. Allow the mittens to dry before handling. Glue a piece of ribbon or yarn to each mitten and tie them together.

54

Art for the Birds

Tools and Materials

Crayons
Shoebox lid
Flour
Water
Sunflower and bird seed
Yarn or cord

Activity

Give each child a shoebox lid. Encourage them to make simple designs in the shoebox lids with crayons. Make a paste with the flour and water. Cover the design with sunflower and bird seeds. Punch two holes at the top of the box lid and thread yarn through to make a hanger. Hang this art from a favorite tree limb and watch the birds visit daily.

55

Tall Dragon Shaker

Tools and Materials

Two heavy duty paper plates
Sketch of a dragon face
Paint
Crayons and markers
Scissors
Glue
Crepe-paper streamers
Rice, dried beans, or pebbles
Stapler
Long dowel stick
Heavy tape

Activity

Ask the children to paint the outsides of the two paper plates. Color the pattern of the dragon with crayons or markers. When the plates are dry, cut out and glue the dragon face in the middle of one plate. Place a handful of beans in the center of one plate and staple the two plates securely together. Staple crepe-paper streamers around the edges of the plate. With heavy tape, attach a thin wooden dowel to the back plate. Have the children march around the room, moving their shakers up and down to celebrate the holiday.

pattern

56

Reproducible

Parade Mask

Tools and Materials

Paper plate
Scissors
Paint
Glue
Paintbrushes
Collage trims (feathers, yearn, cotton balls, straw or raffia, sequins, buttons, ribbons, etc.)
Crayons or markers
Hole punch

Activity

Masks are part of the parade celebrations during the Chinese New Year. Give each child half of a paper plate. Encourage them to paint the surface any color. When the plate is dry, invite each child to draw a face and glue on all kinds of fancy decorative trims. With the hole punch, make a hole on each side of the plate, then thread a ribbon through each hole. Place the mask on the child's face and tie the ribbons around the head.

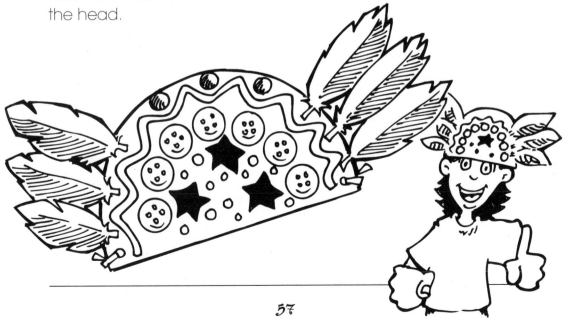

57

Red Lanterns

Tools and Materials

Red construction paper
Crayon
Scissors
Stapler or tape

Activity

Fold a 9" x 12" (22.5cm x 30cm) piece of red construction paper in half lengthwise. Red is the good luck color for this holiday. Draw five lines about an inch (2.5cm) apart from the fold line to about ½ inch (1.25cm) from the edge. Open the page and ask the children to decorate the blank side with crayons. Encourage them to use traditional Chinese designs of the New Year celebration like fireworks, flowers, dragons, lions, and masks. Fold the paper to show the lines and cut from the fold to one inch (2.5cm) from the opposite edge. Turn the paper around to show the design. Roll the paper lengthwise into a tube and staple or tape the edges together. Make a handle from a construction-paper strip and attach it to the top.

Hang the lanterns from the ceiling around the room.

58

© Fearon Teacher Aids • FE7950

Fortune Balloons

Tools and Materials

Red balloons
Strips of white paper
Pen or marker
Wooden toothpicks

Activity

Ask the children to write good luck fortunes, positive thoughts, and nice wishes on strips of white paper. Fold the strip into a small enough piece to fit into the mouthpiece of a balloon. Blow up the balloons and tie knots in the ends. Store the balloons in a big box or trash bag. When it's time to celebrate the Chinese New Year, give each child a balloon. Encourage everyone to shout "Gung Hay Fat Choy" ("Happy New Year" in Chinese). Have children pop their balloons with a toothpick. Invite each child to read his or her fortune aloud. All of the children should be delighted with a special fortune or a treat.

Caution: Carefully supervise the popping of the balloons. Immediately gather and discard the toothpicks and deflated balloons.

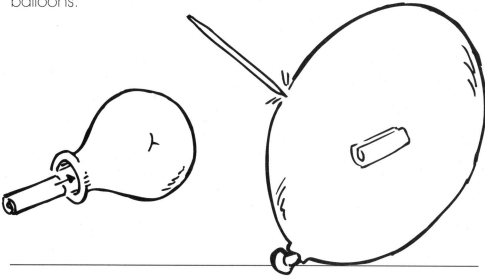

Patriotic Money Rubbings

Tools and Materials

White copy paper
Crayons or colored pencils
Various coins (penny, nickel, dime, etc.)

Activity

Place a piece of white copy paper over a penny. Use the side of a crayon to do a coin rubbing. Use a quarter to make a rubbing of George Washington. Continue with different coins using different colors for each coin. Make a colorful collage of coin rubbings.

George Washington Hat

Tools and Materials

Red, white and blue construction paper
Stapler
Crayons or markers
Sticker stars

Activity

Fold a piece of 8½" x 11" (21.3cm x 27.5cm) construction paper crosswise into three equal parts. Cut on the folds. Staple each piece together (end to end) to form a triangular-shaped hat. Decorate with sticker stars and color a cherry sprig in the corner of one strip.

Recite this traditional chant as you march around the room wearing this hat:

My hat, it has three corners (point to triangle hat)
Three corners has my hat.
If it did not have three corners (raise three fingers)
It would not be my hat. (shake head sideways)

Washington's Cherry Tree

Tools and Materials

Small twigs
Red dot stickers
Construction paper
Glue

Activity

Talk about the famous story of George Washington's honesty in cutting down the cherry tree. Then take the children on a nature walk to collect small twigs. In the classroom, glue the twigs securely onto construction paper. Stick the red dots along the twig as cherries. Arrange some stickers randomly on the page as if they had fallen from the tree.

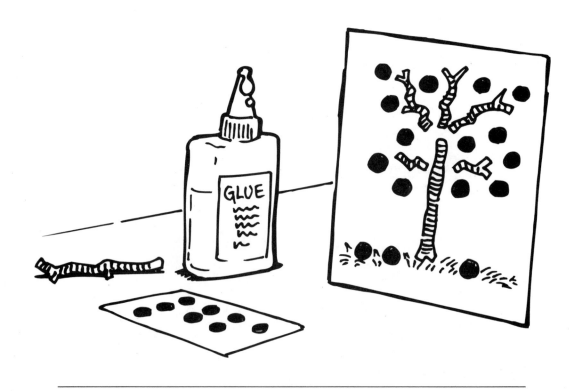

Presidential Tube Puppets

Tools and Materials

Cardboard toilet-paper tube
Markers and crayons
Sketches of Presidents Washington and Lincoln
Scissors
Glue

Activity

Duplicate the sketches of the Presidents to fit onto a toilet-paper tube. Invite the children to color, cut, and glue the Presidential sketches to the tube. Glue one President to the front side and the other President to the back. Once completed, this puppet can be manipulated by placing the tube over two or three fingers.

63

Mr. Valentine

Tools and Materials

Red construction paper
Rubber bands
Scissors
Stapler
Markers and crayons

Activity

Cut six hearts from red construction paper. A large heart for the body, a smaller heart for the head, and four very small hearts for the hands and feet. Cut a rubber band into several pieces. Staple the ends of the rubber-band pieces to the hands and feet. Staple the opposite ends to the body. In the same way, attach the head to the body. Staple a whole rubber band to the top of the head. Use markers to draw facial features and decorations.

Red-Colored Glasses

Tools and Materials

Cardboard or poster board
Red cellophane
Tape or glue
Chenille stems
Crayons and markers
Stapler
Hole punch

Activity

Cut heart-shaped frames out of cardboard (pattern below).
Assist the children to cut along the dotted lines to make eye
holes. Decorate the frames with the crayons and markers.
Tape or glue red cellophane and insert chenille stems. Punch
holes on both sides of the frames, and insert chenille stems.
Bend the chenille stems over the child's ears to fit. Ask the
children to describe how things look different when wearing
their red Valentine glasses.

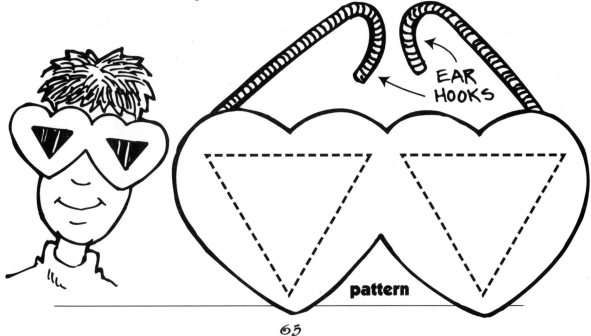

EAR HOOKS

pattern

65

Food Valentine Cards

Tools and Materials

Canned-food labels from vegetables and fruit
Construction paper
Glue
Markers and crayons

Activity

Cut out pictures from canned vegetable and fruit labels. Pictures can also be found on food boxes, magazines, and catalogs. Fold a sheet of construction paper in half to make a card. Glue the food pictures on the front cover. Inside write a cute caption and deliver this valentine to a special someone.

Food Label Captions:

"You're the Apple of My Eye." (glue a picture of an apple)
"Peas Be My Valentine." (glue a picture of peas)
"My Heart Beets for You." (glue a picture of beets)
"We'd Be a Great Pear." (glue a picture of a pear)
"Orange You Glad You're Mine?" (glue a picture of an orange)

Love for the Birds

Tools and Materials

Stale bread
Heart cookie cutter
Peanut butter
Birdseed
Chenille stem

Activity

Invite the children to cut heart shapes with a Valentine cookie cutter out of stale bread. Spread peanut butter on each piece; then sprinkle it with birdseed. Make a hole at the top and insert a chenille stem for a hanger. Hang this bird treat from trees outside the classroom.

Mr. Tooth Puppet

Tools and Materials

Brown lunch bag
White construction paper
Glue
Crayons and markers

Activity

On white construction paper, draw Mr. Happy Tooth with happy eyes and a big smiling mouth. Cut Mr. Tooth in half, crosswise just under the crown. Glue the crown of the tooth to the end flap of a brown paper bag and place the root part just under the flap of the bag. Encourage children to manipulate this bag puppet and let "Mr. Happy Tooth" talk and sing.

68

Spring

Spring is a time of rebirth that comes with warmer weather, wind and rain. Spring arrives between winter and summer, usually on March 20th with the Vernal Equinox. The beauty of nature comes alive as the budding of plants appears and the animals return. This is a wonderful time of year with colorful holidays and outdoor activities.

Rubber-Band Pictures

Tools and Materials

Rubber bands of different sizes and colors
Glue
Paper
Crayons or markers

Activity

Give the children an assortment of rubber bands of different colors and sizes. Encourage them to glue them onto paper making designs like flowers, insects, trees, clouds, rainbows, and kites. Enhance the rubber-band designs by coloring them with crayons and markers.

70

Wooden Glider

Tools and Materials

Two wooden tongue depressors
Tempera paint (any color)
Blue construction paper
White chalk or cotton
Glue

Activity

Give two wooden tongue depressors to each child. Paint these sticks any color. When dry, glue the tongue depressors (one across the other) onto the blue construction paper. Draw billowing clouds on the picture. Glue cotton onto the clouds for texture.

Cotton-Ball Creations

Tools and Materials

1 cup (240ml) flour
1 cup (240ml) water
Food coloring
Cotton balls
Cookie sheet
Oven
Cardboard or wood
Glue

Activity

Cotton ball creations are a form of kitchen art that is fun, colorful, and non-toxic. Mix 1 cup (240ml) flour with 1 cup (240ml) water. Divide this batter into several containers and add food coloring. Coat the cotton balls with the mixture and create designs onto a greased cookie sheet. Make sure all cotton balls touch one another. Bake the completed design in a 275°F (135°C) oven for 50-60 minutes. Make sure the cotton balls have hardened, but do not let them get brown. These baked creations can be mounted onto cardboard or wood with glue.

72

Hairy People

Tools and Materials

Paper cup
Wiggly eyes or buttons
Markers
Glue
Potting soil
Grass seed
Water

Activity

Draw a face onto a paper cup. Glue plastic wiggly eyes or buttons in place. Glue another button for a nose and draw a mouth with a marker. Fill the cup half full with potting soil. Sprinkle grass seed on soil in the cup, then sprinkle a light layer of soil on top. Water the planter and place it in a warm, bright place. Within a week, your special person will grow a head of hair.

73

Sunshine Flower

Tools and Materials

White and green construction paper
Red, yellow, and blue cellophane
Glue or tape
Scissors

Activity

Cut a circle from white construction paper. Attach it to a stem cut from green construction paper. Cut petals from the red, yellow, and blue cellophane. Glue or staple the cellophane petals on the white circle. Slightly overlap the petals to view the different tints of secondary colors.

Bubble Art Prints

Tools and Materials

Bubble solution
Shallow container
Straw
Paper
Food coloring

Activity

Add food coloring to the bubble solution in a shallow container. Using a straw, blow air to produce a froth of bubbles. Carefully lay a white sheet of paper on top of the bubbles. Gently lift up the paper and a print of bubbles will appear.

Variation: Give your bubble print a sea effect by cutting out fish shapes from construction paper and gluing them on randomly.

75

Homemade Bubble Recipe

Tools and Materials

¼ cup (60ml) liquid detergent
½ cup (120ml) water
1 teaspoon (5ml) sugar
Few drops of food coloring (optional)
Shallow container
Paper cup

Activity

Mix all the ingredients together. Place them into a shallow container. Experiment with bubble blowing, using a paper cup with holes in the bottom, a plastic six-pack holder, a plastic berry basket, a funnel, the finger holes in a pair of scissors, and a chenille stem loop. Discover blowing many different shapes and colors of bubbles.

Over the Lucky Rainbow

Tools and Materials

Black construction paper
Chalk or white crayon
Scraps of colorful construction paper
Glue

Activity

On a piece of black construction paper, draw seven arches with chalk or white crayon. Tear small pieces of red, orange, yellow, green, blue, indigo, and violet construction paper. Glue a different color of torn-paper pieces within each arch. Fill in the entire area. Colors of each arch should follow the order of the rainbow—red, orange, yellow, green, blue, indigo, and violet.

77

Shamrock Dessert

Tools and Materials

Vanilla ice cream
Green sugar sprinkles
Licorice

Activity

Children can make and enjoy this fun dessert. Place three small scoops of vanilla ice cream on a plate to look like a shamrock. Sprinkle the ice cream with green sugar sprinkles. Place a licorice piece between the two scoops as a stem.

Shamrock Crown

Tools and Materials

Poster board or cardboard
Green chenille stems
Green construction paper
Stapler
Trims
Marker
Glue or tape

Activity

Measure and cut a band of cardboard to fit around each child's head. Staple the ends together. Attach green chenille stems around the top edge of the crown. Cut shamrock shapes from green construction paper (pattern below). Attach the shamrocks to each chenille stem with tape or glue. Use beads or sequins for sparkle. Personalize the crowns with the child's name and "Happy St. Patrick's Day" written on the band.

← pattern

Reproducible

Hearty Shamrock

Tools and Materials

White paper
Green construction paper
Scissors
Glue
Several colors of construction-paper scraps
Hole punch

Activity

Cut three hearts out of green construction paper. Form a shamrock by gluing the points of the hearts together on a piece of paper. Make a stem from scraps of construction paper and glue it to the shamrock. Decorate the shamrocks with colorful paper confetti glued randomly over the shamrock.

Note: Confetti can be made by punching holes from construction paper with a hole punch.

Weaving Tube

Tools and Materials

Toilet-paper tube
Yarn
Scissors

Activity

Take an empty cardboard toilet-paper tube and cut slits in the
ends. Thread yarn lengthwise between the slits to create a
warp (arrangement of yarns in a loom). Encourage children
to weave yarn over and under the warp around the tube. It
would be easiest to use two different colors of yarns.

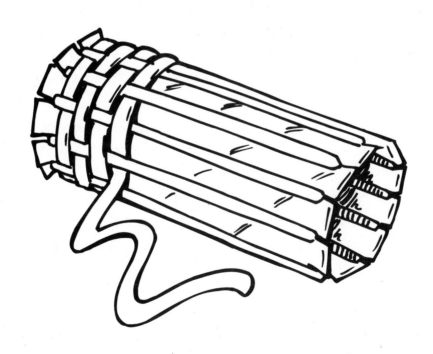

Recycled Wind Sock

Tools and Materials

Coffee can lid
Two colored plastic shopping bags
Scissors
Glue
String or fishing line
Hole punch
Spring-type clothespins

Activity

Cut the bottoms off two plastic bags. Cut down one side of each bag to make two flat pieces of plastic. Cut the center out of a coffee can lid. Place a line of glue around the rim of the lid and start to wrap one of the plastic bags around it. Use spring-type clothespins to hold the plastic in place until the glue dries. Allow to dry before handling. If the glue does not securely hold the plastic, use tape. Form a tube by gluing or taping the sides of the bag together. With the other plastic bag, cut three-inch (7.5cm) wide strips of fringe. Tape or glue the fringe to the bottom of the first bag.

Use a hole punch to make two holes (one across from the other) in the rim of the coffee can lid. Cut a length of string or fishing line and thread it through the holes. Hang the windsock outdoors.

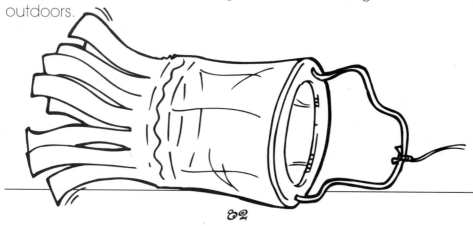

82

3-D Kite Art

Tools and Materials

Construction paper (any color)
Plastic or styrofoam packing pieces
Glue
Scissors
Crayons or markers

Activity

Cut kite shapes from different colors of construction paper.
Glue a plastic packing piece to the back of each shape.
Glue these 3-D kites on construction paper. Draw clouds, the
sun, and birds to create a beautiful sky scene. Remember to
draw ribbon tails at the bottom of each kite!

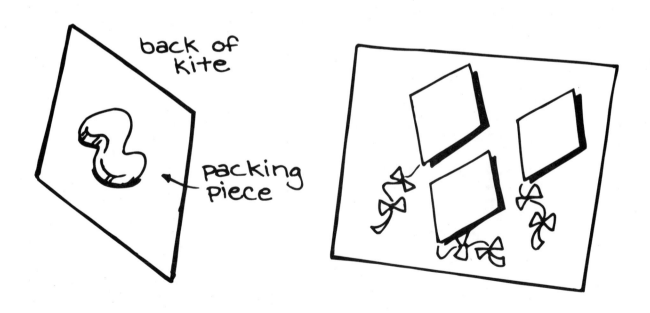

back of
kite

packing
piece

Paper-Plate Kite

Tools and Materials

Paper plate
Stapler
Crepe paper
Yarn or string
Magazine pictures
Scissors
Glue
Crayons and markers

Activity

Decorate a paper plate with any kind of pictures and designs. Use cut out pictures from old magazines or draw your own with crayons or markers. Staple five or six strips of crepe paper to the bottom end of the paper plate. Punch two holes on the opposite side of the plate and tie a piece of yarn for the handle. Encourage the children to run while holding the kite's handle to make it fly behind them.

84

Cut-and-Paste Rabbit

Tools and Materials

Construction paper (any color)
Scissors
Glue
Markers or crayons

Activity

Cut out a large and a medium-size heart from any color of construction paper. Turn the hearts upside down and glue the smaller heart on top of the large heart. Cut two each of arms, legs and ears from construction paper and glue them to your rabbit. Use the drawing below as a guide. Draw in facial features.

85

Margarine Tub Bunny Basket

Tools and Materials

Construction paper (any color)
Scissors
Glue
Empty margarine tub
Chenille stem
Cotton ball

Activity

First punch two holes on opposite sides of a margarine container. A chenille stem makes a great handle. Insert a chenille stem into the two holes and fold the ends to make a handle. Cut a bunny's head from construction paper, using the patterns below. Invite the children to color in all the facial features. Glue the rabbit head onto one side of a margarine tub. Glue a cotton ball to the other side for a tail.

pattern

Reproducible

Candy Bunny

Tools and Materials

Heavy cardboard
Two paper plates
Stapler
Paints, markers, crayons
Tape
Wrapped candy

Activity

Cut a circle larger than a paper plate out of heavy cardboard. This will be the bunny's body. Use one paper plate for the head. Cut two ears from the second paper plate as shown. Assemble all the pieces with a stapler. Using paints, markers, or crayons, draw the bunny's face and ears. Tape wrapped candy all over the body. Display the bunny and encourage students to visit the Candy Bunny and take a sweet treat!

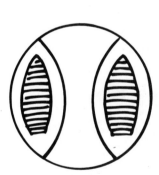

**bunny
ear
pattern**

Easter Egg Wreath

Tools and Materials

Paper plate
Construction paper or wall paper samples
Scissors
Markers, crayons, paint
Glue
Hole punch
Yarn or ribbon

Activity

Cut out the inner circle of a paper plate. Draw and cut egg shapes from various colors of construction paper. Use crayons or paints to decorate the eggs with designs like zig-zags, stripes and polka dots. Glue the decorated eggs onto the wreath part of the paper plate. Make as many eggs as needed to fit completely around the circle. Punch a hole at the top. Use either yarn or ribbon to make a hanger. Display the wreath.

Variation: Pretty patterned eggs can be cut using wallpaper samples.

Flower Glove Puppet

Tools and Materials

Latex glove
Small pompoms (red, blue, purple—the colors of flowers)
Glue
Fiberfill stuffing
Craft stick
Markers
Yarn

Activity

Using the craft stick, stuff a latex glove with fiberfill. Push the stick into the bottom of the glove for a handle and tie the glove closed at the bottom with a piece of yarn. Draw a cute face with permanent markers in the palm of the glove. Glue pompoms onto the top of each finger. Holding the handle move your flower puppet around and recite the Spring poem.

Spring flowers blow in the
    breeze
Sway back and forth and rustle
    their leaves. (move the puppet
    back and forth)
Their pretty colors brighten our
    day (smile)
Let's gather together and
    make a bouquet! (all the
    puppets stand together)

Pebble Basket

Tools and Materials

One tuna can, clean and empty
Heavy craft glue
Aquarium gravel (used in fish tanks)
Ribbon
Potpourri
Colored pantyhose or tulle fabric
Colored rubber bands
Masking tape

Activity

Cover the rim of the aluminum can with masking tape. Then apply a thick coat of craft glue to the outside surface of the can. Roll the can around in a plate of gravel. Make sure all the surface is covered with pebbles. Fill the can with flower petals or ready-made potpourri. Cover the opening by stretching a piece of colored pantyhose or tulle across the top and secure it with a rubber band. Cut a wide ribbon and glue to each side of the can for a handle.

Triangle Basket

Tools and Materials

Construction paper (any color)
Glue
Paper doily
Rickrack trim
Packages of flower seeds

Activity

Cut two pieces of construction paper into triangles. Glue the bottom edges together leaving the top edge open. Decorate by gluing a paper doily on one triangle for the front of the basket. Glue rickrack trim around the edges. For a handle, cut a 7" (24.5cm) strip of rickrack and glue or staple the ends inside the triangle basket. Place a package of flower seeds inside and give this as a May Day gift to friends and neighbors.

© Fearon Teacher Aids • FE7950

Lilies on a Plate

Tools and Materials

White, green, and yellow construction paper
Paper plate
Glue
Scissors
Pencil

Activity

Make a lily by tracing your hand on white paper and cutting it out. Curl the fingers around a pencil to make the petals face the center. For the stamens, cut two strips of yellow paper ¼" (.63cm) wide by 4" (10cm) long. Curl the stamens around a pencil and then glue them to the center of the lily. Glue the entire lily flower in the center of the paper plate. Draw and cut leaves and a stem from the green paper and glue these on the plate.

92

Mexican Tinware

Tools and Materials

Cardboard
Aluminum foil
Glue
Scissors
Markers and paint
Hole punch
Yarn

Activity

Draw a large flower or animal shape onto a piece of cardboard. Carefully cut out the shape. Glue aluminum foil (dull side facing out) to both sides of the cardboard. Use markers or paint to make bold lines and dots to decorate the tinware replica. Punch a hole at the top and thread yarn to use as a hanger or necklace.

Yarn Art

Tools and Materials

Cardboard
Glue
Yarn
Tape
Craft stick

Activity

One a square of cardboard, squeeze a bead of glue in any design. Popular designs used in Mexico are birds, people, fish, and the sun. Take a length of yarn and press it onto the glue, using the craft stick to help arrange the yarn in place. Use many colors and fill in the entire surface of the cardboard. Allow the design to dry thoroughly. Tape a piece of yarn to the back as a hanger.

Fiesta Placemats

Tools and Materials

Construction paper (any color)
Tissue paper (all colors)
Clear adhesive paper
Scissors
Glue

Activity

Make individual placemats for the children to eat their fiesta lunch or snack. Tear or cut small pieces of colorful tissue paper. Glue the pieces onto a sheet of construction paper using the collage method. Cover the entire placemat. When the glue is completely dry, cover the entire mat with clear adhesive paper. Trim off any excess paper. You will now have a very colorful fiesta placemat.

95

Individual Piñatas

Tools and Materials

Brown lunch bag for each child
Old newspaper
Ribbon
Crayons and markers
Construction-paper scraps (any color)
Glue
Wrapped candies

Activity

Encourage each child to make their own piñata to take home and play the game with their families. Decorate the bag with markers and crayons. Glue on the construction-paper pieces to make pretty designs. Stuff the bag with crumpled newspaper. In the middle of the stuffing insert wrapped treats and candies. Gather the open end of the bag together and tightly tie it with ribbons leaving the tails of the ribbons to be used as hangers. Send home an instruction sheet describing how to play the piñata game.

Instructions for Using Piñata

The piñata is hung from the ceiling or a doorway. One player is handed a broomstick, turned around three times and given three attempts to break the piñata. Older children should be blindfolded. Repeat with family members until the piñata is broken and everyone receives a treat.

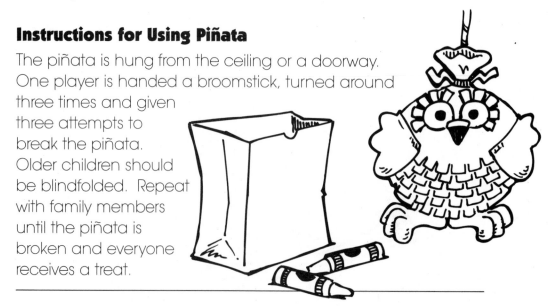

Star Wand

Tools and Materials

Paper-towel tube
Cardboard
Red, white, and blue construction paper
Red, white, or blue poster paint
Glue
Glitter
Ribbons
Stapler
Scissors
Paintbrush

Activity

Paint the paper-towel tube red, white, or blue. Allow the tube to dry thoroughly before handling. Cut different sizes of star shapes from cardboard. Trace and cut out the stars from construction paper. Then glue the construction paper and cardboard stars together to make them sturdier. Decorate the stars with glue starburst designs. Then sprinkle glitter on top of the stars and shake off the excess. Staple the stars to one end of the ribbon and attach the other end to the top of the paper-towel tube. The children can use their wands to whirl the stars as they march around the room to patriotic music.

97

Colonial Flag

Tools and Materials

8½" x 11" (21.3cm x 27.5cm) sheet of paper
Red, white, and blue construction paper
Star stickers

Activity

Cut seven red strips and six white strips of construction paper.
Glue the strips down to the 8½" x 11" (21.25cm x 27.5cm) sheet
of paper starting with red at the top and alternating colors.
Paste a blue square in the upper left-hand corner. Place 13
sticker stars in a circle in the middle of the blue square.

98

Hands Across America

Tools and Materials

White construction paper
Red, white, and blue tempera paint
Black crayons
Brush

Activity

Draw a rough sketch of the United States on white construction paper with black crayon. Brush tempera paint onto the child's hand. Press the hand down onto the paper randomly across the map. Make hand prints in red, white, and blue.

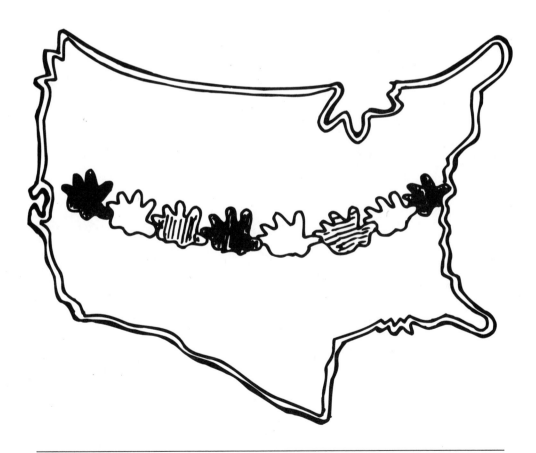

99

A Lovely Bunch of Chores

Tools and Materials

Cone-shaped paper cup
Markers, glitter, trims, etc.
Craft sticks
Construction paper (any color)
Glue
Scissors

Activity

Decorate a cone-shaped paper cup with ink markers, stickers, glitter and trims. Make flower sticks to put inside. Cut flower shapes like tulips and daisies from colorful construction paper. Meanwhile, write "IOU" chores on craft sticks. For example, empty the dishwasher, take out the garbage, vacuum, polish the furniture, and bathe the dog. Attach the flowers on top of the craft sticks with glue. Arrange the flowers in the basket and present them to Mom or someone special.

100

Clothespin Trivet

Tools and Materials

12 Spring-type clothespins
Glue
Heavy cardboard
Stain, varnish, or paint

Activity

Cut a 2-inch (5cm) piece of heavy cardboard for a base. Remove the clips from the clothespins. Glue the flat sides of the wood together around the circular base to form a starburst trivet. Allow the trivet to dry thoroughly before handling. If you like, stain, varnish or paint the wood pieces.

Scarf Holder

Tools and Materials

Cardboard
Wallpaper
Toilet-paper tube
Chenille stems
Glue
Scissors

Activity

Cut a butterfly shape from cardboard (pattern below). Trace and cut out the butterfly pattern from a scrap of wallpaper. Glue the two butterflies together. Cover a toilet-paper tube with the same wallpaper. Glue the tube to the middle of the back of the butterfly. From chenille stems, make a set of antennae to use as hanging hooks. Hang this holder on the wall and pass scarves through the tube.

Note: Use any shape for the scarf holder, such as a heart, flower, or even an animal.

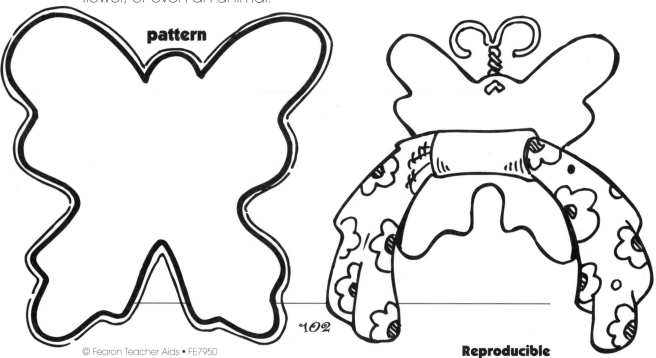

pattern

102

Reproducible

Whimsical Plant Pokes

Tools and Materials

Plastic lids
Permanent markers
Scissors
Craft sticks
Sequins, glitter, or faux gems
Glue

Activity

Cut any type of shape from a recycled plastic lid. Draw happy faces or any picture on the plastic with permanent markers. Glue on sequins, gems, or glitter. Attach the finished shape to a craft stick with glue. Poke the stick into the dirt. Dress up Mom's favorite green plant or even a new one with these cute decorative pokes.

Caution: Supervise children carefully when using glitter.

Bottled Laundry Art

Tools and Materials

Glass jar
Dry laundry detergents (several colors)
Fabric
Ribbon

Activity

Fill a clean and unlabeled glass jar with layers of colored dry laundry detergent. Detergents can be found in white, blue, green, and pink. Carefully make striped layers. Replace the lid on the jar. For a decorative finish, cut a 4" x 6" (10cm x 15cm) circle of fabric and attach it onto the lid with a length of pretty ribbon. This is a pretty as well as useful gift.

Peace Dove

Tools and Materials

White poster board
Markers
Scissors
Glue

Activity

Cut out a bird shape and wing. Draw the eye and beak. Write words of peace using different languages on the wing with markers. Glue the wing to the bird body.

Peace	English
Paix	French
Paz	Spanish
Mup	Russian
Salaam	Arabic

Poppies

Tools and Materials

Red crepe paper
Scissors
Green chenille stem

Activity

Poppies (red flowers) are traditionally given out and worn on Memorial Day to remember the soldiers who died on the battlefields. Cut two circles of crepe paper for each poppy. Lay the circles on top of each other. Poke two small holes in the center of both pieces. Thread the one end of the chenille stem up through one hole, bend it and bring it down through the other hole. Twist the chenille stem to make a stem and secure the flower.

Patriotic Pins

Tools and Materials

Large safety pins
Red, white, and blue plastic beads

Activity

Make these patriotic pins in red, white, and blue to wear on shirts, jackets, and sneakers. Slip the colored beads onto the pin in alternating colors. Carefully pin the safety pin onto your fabric.

Caution: Closely supervise children when working with pins or beads.

Summer

Summer is the time between spring and fall. It usually begins around June 21st, with the summer solstice. Summer is often considered the best season of the year. Usually hot and dry, it is the time for water activities and outdoor fun.

Father's Placemat

Tools and Materials

Construction paper
Crayons or markers
Clear adhesive paper

Activity

Invite each child to draw a picture of his or her father on a sheet of construction paper. At the top print the phrase "Fathers Are Loved All Over the World." Write the foreign words for Father randomly across the paper.

Der Vater	German
Padre	Italian
Pere	French
Padre	Spanish
Bah Bah	Chinese
Patera	Greek

To preserve the placemat, cover with a sheet of clear adhesive paper or laminate.

Photo Tie

Tools and Materials

Old tie
Jar lids
Photos or paper to draw pictures on
Heavy glue

Activity

Ask the childrens' mothers to send in an old tie that Dad will no longer use. Knot these ties in wearable fashion. Glue photos or drawings of special people and events onto each lid. Using three or four lids per tie, use heavy glue to stick the lids onto the front of the tie. Let the project dry thoroughly. Give this gift to a family member as a special photo collage to hang at home or in the office.

Pencil Caddy

Tools and Materials

Empty tin can
Acrylic or spray paint
Spring-type clothespin
Two bottle caps or jug lids
Glue
Black permanent marker
Index card

Activity

Wash out a tin can. Paint it with acrylic or spray paint. Make a "personalized" message keeper for someone special   Glue a spring-type clothespin on the can for a nose. Glue on two bottle caps or jug lids for eyes. With a black permanent marker, draw eyeballs inside the bottle caps and any other desired facial features. Encourage the children to make the can look just like someone special to them. Clamp on a paper message that says "Happy Father's Day—I Love You!" Or "You are special—I Love You!"

Fizz Fun

Tools and Materials

Empty glass bottle
Balloon
Markers
Vinegar
Baking soda

Activity

Draw a happy face on a deflated balloon with markers. With adult supervision, pour one inch (2.5cm) of vinegar into the bottle. Put two teaspoons (10ml) of baking soda inside the balloon. Quickly slip the open end of the balloon over the neck of the bottle. Watch as the gas made from the soda and vinegar inflates the balloon.

Air Boat

Tools and Materials

Half gallon (1.9l) milk or juice carton
Balloon
Scissors
Tub or wading pool of water

Activity

Cut a half gallon (1.9l) milk or juice carton in half lengthwise.
Use one of the halves for each boat you make. Poke a hole in
the center of what used to be the bottom of the milk carton.
Insert a deflated balloon through the hole. Blow up the
balloon, but do not tie the end. Place the boat in a bathtub
or wading pool Release the balloon and watch as the
expelled air moves the boat across the water.

Wave Bottle

Tools and Materials

Small jar
Water
Blue food coloring
Mineral oil

Activity

Fill a small jar about two-thirds full with water. Add a few drops of blue food coloring and shake well. Fill the rest of the jar with mineral oil. Secure the lid well. Encourage the children to roll the jar sideways, gently tipping it to create waves.

114

Fireworks Painting

Tools and Materials

Poster paint in red, white, and blue
Water
Black construction paper
Drinking straw
Three containers

Activity

Using water, thin each color of poster paint in a separate container. Place a large drop of paint onto a piece of black construction paper. Use the drinking straw to blow on each paint drop to create a starburst design. Continue this process with all the colors.

Firecracker

Tools and Materials

Toilet-paper tube
Red construction paper
Yellow yarn
Gold star stickers
Tape or glue
Crayons and markers

Activity

Measure and cut a piece of red construction paper to cover the toilet-paper tube. Before attaching, lay the paper flat and decorate with star stickers, crayons, and markers. Glue or tape the decorated paper on the tube. Glue or tape a short piece of yarn to one end to represent a fuse.

These are wonderful decorations for the classroom tables.

Pompom

Tools and Materials

Toilet-paper tube
Tissue paper
Scissors
Glue
Paint
Paintbrush

Activity

Paint a toilet-paper tube with poster paint and let it dry. Fold a sheet of tissue paper in half lengthwise. Make cuts every 1½" – 2" (3.75cm – 5.0cm) from the cut edge to about 1½" (3.75cm) from the fold to create a fringe. Apply glue along the folded edge and wrap the paper around the tube.

Noise Makers

Tools and Materials

Empty aluminum soft drink cans
Dried beans or raw rice
Heavy tape
Aluminum foil
Decorative stickers

Activity

Use clean aluminum soft drink cans. Place a handful of dried beans or raw rice into the can; tape the opening shut. Cover each can completely with aluminum foil. Decorate the can with sticker stars, flags, and other July Fourth symbols. Shake, shake, shake!

Watermelon Slice

Tools and Materials

Red and green construction paper
Watermelon seeds
Scissors
Glue

Activity

Cut a large half circle out of green construction paper. Glue a slightly smaller half circle of red construction paper on top of the green. This represents a juicy slice of watermelon. Glue real watermelon seeds onto the red slice.

Mr. Sun

Tools and Materials

Paper plate
Yellow tempera paint
Markers
Crepe paper—yellow
Scissors
Stapler, glue, or tape

Activity

Paint a paper plate with yellow tempera paint. When dry, draw on a happy face with markers. Attach short yellow crepe-paper streamers all around the plate with tape, glue, or a stapler. Read the poem as a group.

Oh, Mister Sun, Sun, Mister Golden Sun,
Please shine down on me.
Oh, Mister Sun, Sun, Mister Golden Sun,
Hiding behind a tree.
These little children are asking you,
To please come out so we
*   can play with you.*
Oh, Mister Sun, Sun,
*   Mister Golden Sun,*
Please shine down on me.

120

Fish Net

Tools and Materials

Construction paper
Crayons
Net fabric (from produce bags of oranges and grapefruit)
Tape

Activity

Use crayons to draw underwater objects like fish, sunken ships, and seaweed on light blue construction paper. Cover your drawing with net fabric like tulle or grocery netting. Tape the edges to secure.

Paper-Plate Fish

Tools and Materials

Two Paper plates
Scissors
Stapler
Crayons or markers

Activity

Cut a triangular piece from a paper plate for the mouth of a fish. Staple this same piece to the opposite side of the plate to represent the tail fin. Color the scales and eye.

Variation: Use two small paper plates. Cut the first plate as shown below. For the tail, attach half of the plate to the back of the second plate. Attach quarter pieces to the sides of the plate for fins.

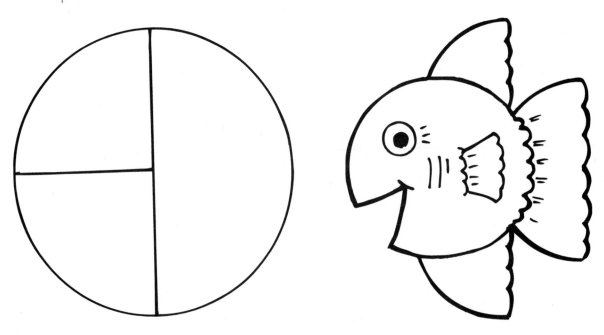

Waterscope

Tools and Materials

Half gallon (1.9l) paper milk carton
Clear plastic wrap
Rubber bands
Scissors

Activity

Cut off the top and bottom of a half gallon (1.9l) paper milk carton. Lay a sheet of clear plastic wrap over one end of he carton. Secure the wrap in place with rubber bands. Place the plastic-covered end of the waterscope into the water and view the sea through the open end.

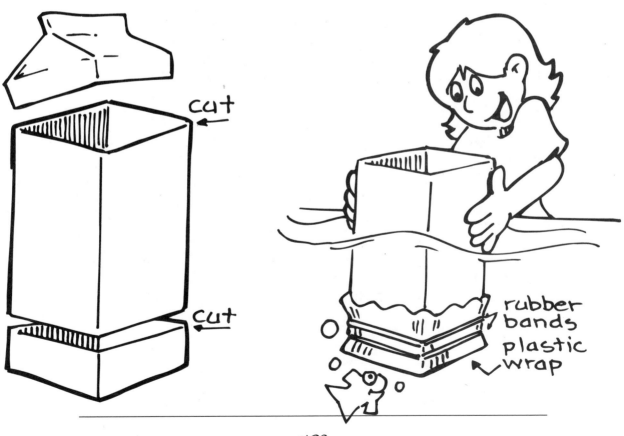

123

Wheel Painting

Tools and Materials

Small toy cars
Tempera paints
Paper

Activity

Gather a few small toy cars. Pour paints (various colors) into shallow containers. Provide a large sheet of paper and invite the children to dip the wheels of the cars into the paint and drive across the page. Encourage them to go forward, backward, and in circles using different colors. Add sound effects and create a zoom-zoom painting.

Glue Painting

Tools and Materials

White liquid glue
Food coloring
Paintbrush
Wax paper (optional)

Activity

Pour white liquid glue into containers. Add a few drops of food coloring to each container and mix. If the glue is too thick to brush, add a few drops of water and mix again. Paint the colored glue on wax paper like tempera paint. After it thoroughly dries, carefully peel the wax paper away from the glue. Hang the glue picture in a window for a see-through effect.

Condensed Milk Painting

Tools and Materials

One can condensed milk
Food coloring
Containers
Cotton-tipped swab
Paper
Paintbrush

Activity

Empty one can of condensed milk into several containers. Add drops of food coloring to tint the milk. Paint on paper using a paintbrush or cotton-tipped swabs. This paint is quite thick. Be aware that this paint medium takes several days to dry, however, the smooth, glossy finish is well worth the wait.

Bag Painting

Tools and Materials

Plastic resealable bag
¼ cup (60ml) finger paint
Heavy tape

Activity

Pour about ¼ cup (60ml) of finger paint (store bought or pudding) into a plastic resealable bag. Seal the top making sure all the air has escaped. It is best to also tape the bag securely. Lay the bag onto the table with paper underneath it. With your fingers, make designs on top of the bag as in regular finger painting. When you tire of this painting, lift the bag so the paint will collect in the bottom. Place the bag down on the paper again and repeat the same procedure for another masterpiece. Using two primary colors in the same bag will mix into a new secondary color. What a great lesson!

127